Racism, Classism, or Just Plain Ignorance

An Examination of the Current Flaws and Failures Inherent in Public Education and Who Is to Blame

Chet Deaver, Ed.D

Copyright © 2020 Chet Deaver

All rights reserved. No part of this publication may be reproduced, stored in a retrieval system, or transmitted in any form or by any means, mechanical, photocopying, recording or otherwise, without prior permission in writing of the author.

ISBN: 9798568363071 (paperback)

Imprint: Independently published

Acknowledgements

It seems that you never really know where to start when writing these very personal words because so many have contributed to the process whether directly or indirectly.

First, and always closest to my heart, I thank my family. They have always understood and supported my reasons for reaching into the depths of some of the topics I choose to champion.

To my Mom ... what an honor it has been to be your son! You made education important to me. You inspired me.

To the many great teachers I have had the great honor of working with over the years. I was always listening, and these words are a reflection of the time we spent together. I am blessed to have had each of you in my professional life.

And finally, to my former students, each of you has had an impact on my life in a way you cannot fathom. I LEARNED FROM YOU! What a concept, huh? I hope that I was able to offer you some direction and guidance in your quest for a quality life.

Table of Contents

Acknowledgements iii

1	History Reveals Itself	1
2	The Problem Grows	6
3	The Problem Persists	8
4	Deficits in Culturally Responsive Education	12
5	It Cannot Be Found in a Book	15
6	Education at a Crossroads	19
7	Perception Is Everything	22
8	It's Broke ... and Needs to be Fixed	27
9	Is Equal Really Equal?	31
10	Now What? Can We Save Our Schools?	34
11	It Will Take Everyone to Make Things Happen	37

References 41

I

History Reveals Itself

The United States Supreme Court's landmark Brown v. Board of Education decision affected both the education of African American students and those responsible for their education. It was the 1950s, and cultural acceptance of the notion that there was a fair and equitable approach to race-related issues with regard to education was stagnant – if it existed at all. Prior to integration, African American students were taught almost exclusively by Black teachers. The decision to desegregate education created a chasm within the system that marked the beginning of the deficit in learning for children of color. Stereotypes were allowed to develop that gave way to a cultural and racial crisis in education. According to research, an actual decline in African American student performance and academic success began with the *Brown* decision. Prior to the *Brown* case, African American children had the unique experience of developing and fostering meaningful and effective relationships with Black teachers. As a result, their learning capabilities were enhanced. An emphasis on reading and arithmetic took precedence over socioeconomic and political concerns. With the desegregation of schools came a division in educational access and understanding that led to disillusionment with the process among Black children. The lack of understanding and acceptance that most children of color experienced in the newly segregated system would create what is now commonly referred to as the "achievement gap." Since the early 1960s, one of the single most challenging issues has been trying to effectively close that gap. Federal guidelines have been implemented. States have prioritized the issue. And yet, sadly, the gap has grown to what is now widely considered to be one of the root causes of systemic erosion in today's educational communities.

Research suggests that the relationships that are developed between teacher and student are paramount to the student's eventual academic success. If, in fact, these relationships are hindered by social malevolence and pedagogical ignorance, then the achievement gap that currently exists between children of color and their White peers will certainly continue to grow. Teacher–student relationships must begin at an early age and continue to develop throughout the educational process. The absence of this type of trust leads to a breakdown in systemic order. When children are left to try to figure out who they are and how they fit into a given situation, bias is allowed to develop, often along the lines of race. This component alone was a driving force in the development of the achievement gap.

RACISM, CLASSISM, OR JUST PLAIN IGNORANCE

The student–teacher relationship is a key component or tenet of culturally relevant teaching and a strong factor in providing academic success or African American students. The *Brown* decision was instrumental in causing the loss of the Black teacher as a significant figure in the educational system due to movements within the school setting to accommodate forced integration. Black teachers were held in high regard by Black parents and the community at large. After integration, they were largely forced to endure emotional stresses and professional hardships that were demoralizing and degrading. Black students suffered as a result of these unfortunate experiences. With the loss of the Black classroom teacher came decades of mistrust and misunderstanding. An age of educational discrimination was born, and the *Brown* decision was at the heart of the problem. Discriminatory practices, whether intended or not, became part of and remain inherent in the practices of today's classrooms.

Conversely, Black children prior to the *Brown* decision were afforded a much more promising approach to teaching and learning. The Supreme Court decision that declared segregated schools to be "inherently unequal" in fact may have contributed to the beginning of what is now considered to be an insurmountable gap in academic achievement. A closer examination of education after *Brown* clearly reveals a system that was ill prepared for the effects of desegregation. With little infrastructure and no financial support, the decision to provide equality was in fact the vehicle that drove much inequality.

When Oliver Brown took his plight, and the ensuing fight, to the Topeka School Board, he couldn't know that the end result would become such a divisive tool in education. His argument that the segregation of public schools violated the Equal Protection Clause of the United States Constitution created an encouragement for change in systemic practices. However, his complaints were based largely on the structural aspects of segregated education, such as transportation and classrooms, and less on the actual opportunities for a quality learning experience. The argument intended to create better buildings and better transportation. What it did instead was allow for a fracturing of a system that was successful. A member of the plaintiff group, Silas Fleming, may have summed up the situation as succinctly as any when he proclaimed that he was "craving light – the entire colored race is craving light, and the only way to reach the light is to start our children together in their infancy and they come up together." Fleming's argument was that separating children at a young age educationally perpetuated a social stigma of being second class. Fleming stated that he didn't want to cast any insinuations that Black teachers are not capable of teaching our children because they are supreme, extremely intelligent and are capable of teaching my kids or White kids or Black kids. The ultimate goal was to allow for the desegregation of schools to occur naturally over a period of time. The goal was to provide for an equal education while desegregation could take place. What happened was the forced movement of children from a place of comfort and concern to one of discord and disdain.

Ultimately, a ruling in favor of the plaintiff validated the concern that segregation of White and Black children in public schools has a detrimental effect upon the colored children. The impact was greater when it had the sanction of law; for the policy of separating the races was usually interpreted as denoting the inferiority of the Black group. A sense of inferiority affected the motivation of a child to learn. Segregation with the sanction of law, therefore, had a tendency to retard the educational and mental development of Black children and to deprive them of some of the benefits they would have received in a racially integrated school system. With this ruling, change in public schools was ushered in, but not without discord and discontent.

When Chief Justice Earl Warren issued his interpretation of the landmark Supreme Court ruling, he declared that separate educational doctrines for White and Black children had no place in society. What he could not know at the time was that the mandate of integration in the public school classroom would create an achievement gap that would continue to grow for decades to come. His call for educational justice would give way to a myriad social injustices that would grow at an alarming rate.

2

The Problem Grows

The political atmosphere in this country has grown into a rage fueled by conceptualizations of racism, classism, and social and cultural discourse. Politicians are more focused on winning the next election than legislating policy for the day. Public perception polls have taken over the rightful place of the political process. Opinions, not facts, rule and control the actions of the moment. Public officials have bowed to greed and power and the opportunities to line their own pockets, always at the expense of the masses.

Tragically, the plight of our children and their education has been overwhelmingly disregarded by the political system. The schools have been neglected, through the lack of or complete loss of funding to the absolute and outright destruction of the system by way of the courts. This has left most of our children alone to face their lives. They are often ill-equipped to face the cultural inequalities that have been created by a broken system. Faced with these facts, how can we expect our children to grow and thrive and to become vibrant members of our society?

RACISM, CLASSISM, OR JUST PLAIN IGNORANCE

Race continues to be the single most explosive issue in American life. These are frightening and uncertain times for our country. As we watch the fast-paced changes coming on almost a daily basis, we remain grossly unprepared for those changes. Our children will suffer the brunt of these social, cultural, and educational ills. The issues of stagnating schools and broken promises have paralyzed our nation and allowed the ignorance of hate, idolatry, and self-absorption to take over. As a people, we must embrace our diverseness, our differences of opinion, and become inclusive and collaborative in spirit and in practice.

3
The Problem Persists

Unsubstantiated and inaccurate thoughts about African American male students and their respective abilities in the classroom have been allowed to permeate today's public school systems. Often these inaccuracies are a result of a total misunderstanding of the culture within the African American community, and Black males are at a disadvantage because of certain traditional perceptions. Common labels placed on these students include criminals and troublemakers and of being prone to violence. As a result of these stereotypical labels, the teaching profession, and education in general, has relegated itself to the stagnation and segregation that was public education prior to the *Brown* decision. Public education must establish a clear understanding that the cultural influences of race, ethnicity, and socioeconomic status are barriers to academic achievement and should begin to develop a real and positive approach to change.

Developing and understanding the explanation for the gap in academic achievement between African American students and their nonminority peers is a key component of the success or failure of any program that targets the gap. African American students comprise approximately 17 percent of the student population in the United States, yet less than 6 percent of the professional teaching force is African American. With almost 85 percent of the teaching population being nonminority (White) females, the likelihood that a young African American male student will encounter a nonminority female as his teacher is high.

Much of the research in this field has indicated that one of the most important considerations in defining a successful nonminority female teacher in the classroom is their "colorblindness." The duality comes in, then, when nonminority female teachers claim, "I don't see color. I see children." In fact, as they do not recognize the cultural individuality of their minority students, nonminority teachers continue to effectively deny the vast differences that race plays in education. Providing a culturally effective academic setting for African American male students is essential to establishing relevance and meaning in the classroom.

Statistics continue to reveal that African American students, particularly males, consistently perform below their White counterparts. According to assessment data, the achievement gap between African American students and their nonminority peers continues to widen as they move through the grade levels of formal education. These statistics provide insight into why additional research is needed to develop strategies that will assist nonminority female teachers in helping African American male students become more academically successful and thereby close the achievement gap. These ideologies have permeated the field and created negative impressions in the professional teaching field, indicating that there remains a need to continue to investigate the challenges that nonminority female teachers face in helping their at-risk African American male students close the academic achievement gap.

Statistically, Black students, specifically males, perform consistently below their nonminority counterparts in reading and math, as indicated by the National Assessment Educational Progress (NAEP) assessments. As much as a 26-point gap was revealed in the reading scores between nonminority and African American students. Closing this gap requires early identification of a problem and the employment of effective teaching practices. However, according to researchers, this is rarely what happens. Consequently, research clearly defines the need for enhanced relevance, rigor, responsiveness, and establishing of positive relationships as a foundation of student achievement, especially young African American male students.

Understanding the limiting factors that cultural theories imply is essential to determining the success of certain classroom teachers. The collateral damage that is caused by the intrusive nature of the culturally deficit teaching has to be understood and addressed, especially by nonminority teachers, if any measure of success in the classroom is to be experienced. The widespread underachievement among students of color and students from lower socioeconomic strata in schools as a result of pervasive racism within the institution is positively identified and explained by the culturally irresponsible institutions such as today's public school systems.

4

Deficits in Culturally Responsive Education

Culturally deficient education theories attribute students' lack of educational success to characteristics often rooted in their cultures and communities and within a system empowered by a lack of understanding and bias. This concept of cultural deficit in learning is grounded in the idea that certain cultures have inherent deficiencies and a diminished ability to achieve. Often, individuals from diverse cultural backgrounds are regarded as intellectually inferior, and there is an overwhelming justification to stereotype these individuals as under-achieving.

When applying culture to education, the goal is to develop attitudes, skills, and an overall ability to function within a system where multicultural ramifications exist. Culture consists of the behavior patterns, symbols, institutions, and other human-made components of the society one lives in. Disqualifying those identifying factors is a leading contributor to the perpetuation of inferior academic practices for minority children in public education.

Applying the influences of family and culture in a responsive and responsible way is paramount to establishing success in closing the achievement gap between African American students, particularly young males, and their White counterparts. The Black family structure is seen as a pivotal point in this process. The decline of the traditional family, due to the lack of a male presence, is seen as a profound influence on the achievement of young Black males. For reasons still not clearly understood in the professional community, this segment of the education population continues to stand out in a negative and disheartening way.

A significant amount of energy needs to be placed in understanding the environmental and cultural factors that influence the way Black male students come to perceive education. Additionally, there remains a need to establish the correlation between those perceptions and their influence on performance and behavior in school. Examining these students' support structure, academic background, and self-efficacy through research measures is essential to understanding where specific systemic flaws may exist. Simply put, we cannot effectively teach what we do not truly understand.

Esteemed author Dr. Cornel West so aptly discussed the effects of poverty on family structures, health care, and education and how the general lack of opportunity for the Black community has overwhelmingly perpetuated the stagnation of the Black man's ability to achieve. The discussion of continued inequities and "benign neglect" of certain administrations from as early as Kennedy through Reagan conveys a historical denial of the systemic ills of the Black community. Gaps in education and literacy gave way to gaps in income and potential. Without addressing and effectively acknowledging a system that is inherently flawed, the likelihood that young African American children, especially males, will succeed educationally is greatly diminished.

5

It Cannot Be Found in a Book

One of the most disparaging aspects of the nonminority classroom teacher is their general lack of true cultural awareness and understanding. Current research suggests that teachers cannot teach what they do not know. Imagine a teacher, trained in a specific content area, who knows the subject matter but knows absolutely nothing about the students in the class. A disconnect is inherently formed, and true learning cannot effectively take place. Unless the teacher becomes acutely aware of specific learning styles, inspirations, needs and interests, obstacles and distractions, and cultural realities, stagnation will prevail. Accordingly, a White teacher most assuredly does not fully understand or comprehend the life of a young Black student, particularly a young Black male. Because of this disconnect, it is entirely likely that the same White teacher cannot effectively "teach" or "reach" the student of color.

Building strong, lasting relationships is the key

to making "learning" happen. William Ward quotes, "Mediocre teachers tell; good teachers explain; superior teachers demonstrate ... but Great teachers inspire!" As rudimentary as it sounds, students must actually "like" you if they are to do well in class. This is even more profound for young Black male students. If they do not sense you truly care and understand them, they will continue to guard themselves against any possibility of being let down. Interactions outside the classroom are often the catalysts to developing strong, understanding relationships. Places like the cafeteria, the playground, and the hallways ... all can be areas where significant engagement takes place. A great classroom teacher must be willing to make adjustments to the classroom to motivate and allow students to excel.

In the movie *Dead Poets Society*, Robin Williams's character immediately senses the lack of inspiration his students have. He "sees" their boredom and overall disdain for the subject matter. Only when he implements some truly unconventional methods does he earn the trust he needs from his students to fully inspire them with content and material he teaches! This same approach is what is required when motivating Black students, particularly young Black males, to succeed academically. They must trust that the system understands and accepts them. They must trust that their goals in life are important and meaningful.

Very often, developing specific "styles" to implement in the classroom is the key to success. But these styles must be inclusive of many aspects. A great teacher must take an inventory of numerous items before he or she can tailor a style worthy of their young African American male students. A great teacher should understand and have a working knowledge of home life, neighborhood issues and concerns, peer pressures, overall interests and interest in the subject matter, instructional methodologies, and the general level of comprehension each student has. There is no "one-size-fits-all" strategy for a classroom. Culturally responsive teachers must recall that, for African American male students, learning is equated with activity, and the role of being a passive participant can be detrimental. Strategies must incorporate a joint collaborative activity between student and teacher that will allow for successful instruction and the building of a positive and productive rapport. The personal beliefs of the classroom teacher could have a profound impact on the achievement ability of the minority student. The teacher who believes he or she can have a positive influence on student achievement, regardless of previous limitations, will inspire the Black student to achieve.

The teacher who refuses to accept the litany of ignorance and apathy regarding Black students and embraces the students' learning capabilities will demand the completion of educational tasks using higher order thinking skills. An attitude of understanding, support, and encouragement is essential to achievement and to opening up a functional dialogue between African American male students and their nonminority teachers. There is a process for understanding the African American student, and it begins with a change in attitude by the teacher. Teachers are required to examine their own image of the student. Next, teachers must make an honest effort to understand the African American culture. A significant moment in this process is the reevaluation of perceptions about African American students. Finally, classroom teachers who are responsive to the cultural diversity of today's school system must conduct purposeful dialogues with African American male students to enhance communications skills rather than depending upon drill-type activities with an overabundance of rules and regulations. According to research, African American students do not incorporate abstract ideas easily. Therefore, teachers should develop strategies which illustrate the abstractions, regulations, and verbal discussions being presented. Incorporating the cultural experiences of the students into the lessons will help make the material relevant as well.

6

Education at a Crossroads

The crisis in professional education awareness has led to the challenges encountered in today's classrooms that emphasize the importance for culturally sensitive and culturally diverse educators. There is an increasing importance for culturally sensitive and culturally diverse educators in today's classroom. Underachievement among students of color and those from lower socio-economic strata in school is a result of pervasive racism within the educational setting. Teachers form low expectations of African American students based on their social, cultural, or economic environment. This viewpoint leads to a failure in responding to the unique needs of students from diverse cultural backgrounds. For too long, these models have absolved schools from their role in the issue of poor academic achievement and shifted the blame almost entirely on the students and their families. Conventional wisdom suggests that the school is simply a place of "teaching and learning," and all other aspects of raising a child should be left to the family. Structurally, this is not possible. When the average educator spends as much or more time with today's children than the traditional family does, it is not only important but also imperative that they take on a surrogate role in the student's development.

Today's public education system is tragically broken. It has become an overly politicized, increasingly over-litigated system that bends to numerical tendencies and arbitrary scoring rather than developing programs and processes that are designed to increase the academic prowess of the students they serve. Legislators argue over how best to "fix" existing problems. Largely, the trend has been to scrap the current way teachers educate in the public system and simply "adopt" new ways of thinking and doing. Charter schools and school vouchers appear to be the newest way to achieve the desired successes. But, with specific criteria in place, many of these programs inherently deny children of color, lower socioeconomic stature, and rural locations the same or similar opportunities as provided to their White, more affluent peers.

From 1973 through 2008, African American children made significant gains in their effort to close the achievement gap. Public schools often made important strides in this area. With the onset of the charter school system, the gap has again become more statistically relevant than in prior years. Unfortunately, as the numbers unfold, African American male students have made less of an impact on those gains as a whole. Data reveals that

RACISM, CLASSISM, OR JUST PLAIN IGNORANCE

the percent change in academic gains from 2008 to 2013 was statistically nonexistent. The current stagnation in academic progress for African American male students clearly defines the need for enhanced relationships between students and teachers. Public school systems should again be held accountable through the NCLB Federal Education Act. Educational communities, especially the classroom teacher, have to place a deliberate and intense focus on redirecting the path of young African American males in an effort to become statistically acceptable. This statute still has no significant process in place to address the systemic barriers of race, culture, and academic segregation that persist in the public system. A combined effort of leadership, resources, and action is needed to ensure an opportunity for academic success for African American male students.

Critical issues facing young Black males include low graduation rates, high rates of special education placement, and a disproportionate use of suspensions and expulsions as a means of discipline. Black males face a tremendous amount of negative social stigma as well. For more than 25 years, Black males have suffered the indignation of social, educational, and economic stagnation, far more than any other race or gender. A sobering statistic is that they are far more likely to attend schools in spite of greater racial segregation and fewer financial resources. This exacerbates an already critical situation facing these young men as they enter the most formative years of their lives.

7

Perception Is Everything

School systems serving high percentages of minorities are far more likely to omit courses with higher rigor than those with higher populations of White students. Less than a third of the high schools with a mostly African American student population offer calculus, and only 40 percent offer physics. Statistics show that more than 80 percent of African American male students recommended for special education services were below grade level in reading ability. Minority students tend to learn material in the classroom far more effectively when teachers utilize a variety of techniques. There are a disproportionate number of Black students failing academically. Recent reports indicate that 28 percent fewer Black males than White males graduated high school. This disparity has been coined the "achievement gap" by education professionals. According to the U.S. Department of Education, the achievement gap is the difference in academic performance between ethnic groups. This definition of the achievement gap has been accepted for decades, but studies suggest that it is problematic because it compares the performance of African American students to subjective standards, thereby excluding multiple aspects of potential barriers to success. There is absolutely no denying that with the onset of "desegregation," the children of color in this country have suffered academically.

Despite the definition of the achievement gap any one group adheres to, there is a disparity in the academic outcome of Black males and other student populations. This phenomenon has concerned researchers for many years. Studies have noted that science and scientific research developed theories to explain the mental inferiority of the Black student. It can be noted that the early works of researchers such as Rita Dunn suggested a biological explanation for specific inferiorities. However, subsequent research on cognitive ability and racial differences has concluded that the perceived mental incapacity of Black males is incorrect. As a result, researchers began to focus on alternate hypotheses including the role of the individual, family, and school environment to explain racial gaps in academic performance. According to research, the problem not only persists but also has become more pervasive than ever.

Cultural settings and significant studies suggest that Black people are often blamed for their plight, yet they are the only racial group that did not come to America voluntarily looking for a better life. Evaluating the importance of the relationship between African American male students and their White teachers is at the root of the cultural relevance argument. The concept of equating differences with deficiencies must cease in practice before true cultural acceptance can occur. The synthesis of two distinctly different cultures, that of the African American and that of the male, yields a wholly separate and identifiable structure of the Black male culture. The distinctness of these dimensions has created a lack of empowerment within the culture, and the educational system continues to perpetuate this lack of power.

The four basic issues of academic relevance for the African American male student are that it is not good to make high grades, they have no control over their academic destiny, they lack a feeling of acceptance within the system, and the ever-present awareness of discrimination issues. To address these issues, the classroom teacher, especially those from outside the shared cultural background, must establish trust and rapport that will eliminate the affront to the student's personal academic integrity. Perception is everything.

Another important aspect of the growing decline of the public school system and the failure of the Black male student is accepting the myth that low-income students who are inherently less likely to succeed academically has exacerbated an-already inflamed problem of statewide educational inequity. Today's educator must be enlightened about the concept that even children from a poverty background have a strong desire to learn. The concept of classism is pervasive when associated with educational disparity. Historically, the concept of poverty and socioeconomics has emerged as a cultural paradigm, which continues to sabotage the educational efforts of minority children. White is seen as privileged and Black is seen as neglected. Because of this stereotypical view, the effects of racial segregation in education continue to grow. Having a segment of society that is disproportionately undereducated is problematic. Current data supports the assertion that the likelihood of being or becoming underemployed or unemployed, and subsequently living in low-income or poverty conditions, is greatly increased because of educational deficiencies. As recently as 2009, 25.8 percent of Blacks were impoverished, compared to 9.4 percent of Whites. Perhaps more telling, 61 percent of Black children live in low-income households, a significantly higher occurrence than the 27 percent of White children from low-income households. Perception is everything.

Another issue at the root of the economic barrier in education is parental involvement. Low-income parents are less likely to be involved in their children's education. The problem is that schools fail to take the issue of socioeconomics into account when planning for family involvement. The malady of economic barriers continues to sabotage the educational achievements of African American males. Economic instability, breakup of the traditional family, and routinely ineffective leadership of the neighborhood system have created a chasm in the development of the African American male.

Economic adversity and the fact that many young

males are forced to work in addition to going to school have a negative impact on academic performance. Current research suggests that African American male students attending high school are at a definite disadvantage academically because of their social, economic, and family situations. These disadvantages are often used as a reference point in the explanation for why African American students perform below their nonminority peers. Perception is everything.

Researchers have argued that Black males are at a disadvantage because of certain traditional perceptions. It is also noted that common labels placed on these students include that of being called criminals and troublemakers and of being prone to violence. As too often African American male students maintain an intense and perpetual state of awareness, their racial identities and Blackness are under constant scrutiny. These types of stereotypical labels have added to the problems that have allowed some of the "woke" ideas of today to emerge. Perception is everything.

8

It's Broke ... and Needs to be Fixed

The "wokeness" our country is experiencing today will ultimately permeate the hallways and classrooms of our public school systems. In fact, with the constant fight over "4 core curriculum" and the new fad of the militant "1619 Project," schools are increasingly being forced to accept the nuances of the day. Sadly, when politicians, lawyers, and radical pundits attempt to direct the dialogue of academics and education, the losers will certainly be the children in our school systems. And, given the current racial tensions being exacerbated by and through an ever-vilifying media and social media outlets, the likelihood that our children of color will experience more difficulties in the public education system is growing.

School systems are, at least in part, absolved from their responsibilities to educate all students, and the charge is shifted almost entirely on the students and their families. Eliminating the need to "fix" African

American students and instead address ways to reach them academically is the only way to stop the culture of classism within the educational system. Diverse student populations are underserved by our educational system and responsible leadership. The study of the ongoing disconnect among cultural awareness of diversity issues, the personal and professional beliefs held collectively, and how those are reflected in teaching practices may lend insight as to what effect these constructs have on holding students back. However, allowing these tragic ideas of "colonialism" and "White privilege" to become part of our public education systems will lead to their premature demise. Our system is flawed. It is broken. "And trending as we are in the direction we are currently in, it will surely destroy any possibility that the public system can survive.

Culturally relevant teaching and the characteristics of academic success for African American male students are more important than ever before. The average teacher, a White female from a middle-class family, misunderstands the dynamics of poverty in relation to education. Thus, without proper training and resources, the teacher will not be able to sustain a positive relationship with these students, regardless of relevant content knowledge. Culturally relevant teachers see their duties and practices as professionals to be a connection between the community and their classrooms. Teaching practices that include culturally relevant connections have to be cultivated in order to help close the achievement gap.

According to researchers, these are rare qualities among nonminority female teachers.

The quality of education that most African American children receive today is far below that of their nonminority peers. The disparaging fact is that Black children are being educated by schools that do not or cannot administer to their specific needs. Instead, they (public schools) deliver the girls to public assistance and the boys to unemployment and incarceration. By developing culturally responsive teaching practices, more opportunities for educational empowerment of marginalized minority students can occur. Research has indicated for decades that there is a specific need for explicit pedagogical practices that teachers should adhere to when working with culturally diverse populations.

According to recent studies, the goals and objectives needed as part of a culturally relevant curriculum include developing awareness and respect for the differences and similarities among diverse groups; promoting sensitivity to and understanding of diverse ethnicities and cultures through exposure to different cultural perspectives; helping students recognize and understand the values and experiences of one's own ethnic and cultural heritage; and identifying, challenging and dispelling ethnic and cultural prejudice, stereotyping, and discrimination in behavior, textbooks, and other instructional materials. It is clear that our public systems are flawed and in many ways antiquated. However, with the current trends moving toward a more radical view of instruction, and with the creation and growth of the charter school system, public education must develop and reinvest in the systemic changes needed to become socially, academically, and racially relevant to survive.

9

Is Equal Really Equal?

Equity in education has long been an ideal. It has been celebrated in a variety of contexts, too. Historically, our founders celebrated education as an ideal – something they envisioned every citizen ought to be entitled to. Unfortunately, though, the practice of equity in education has been less than effective. Equity, in the end, is a difficult ideal to maintain, and many strategies attempting to maintain it have fallen far short in the implementation. As noted in earlier chapters, the Brown v. Board of Education action was in part brought about to achieve some form of equity in the educational process. What happened instead was complete disillusionment with the process and the loss of an ideal to legislative guidelines and judicial reviews with little focus on educational equity.

To achieve true equity, school systems need to adopt an approach to analyzing findings about the recommended shifts in learning approaches and objectives. These approaches should also help teachers and administrators understand not what they have to avoid but what it is that they can do to achieve optimal equity moving forward. Addressing racism in education is the most pressing equity issue public schools are facing, both in Texas and across the country. Racism is the root of so many inequitable policies and practices, and it can no longer be ignored. It permeates our classrooms, our curriculum, and all of the systems that support schools. As advocates, stakeholders must work to include policies and practices that dismantle systems of oppression and that ensure equitable treatment and access to resources and opportunities for students of color. Given the opportunities that public systems do provide, the foundation for success is in place. However, when outside forces are allowed to dictate how these systems are utilized, often the results can be skewed or diminished. In a profession increasingly full of angst and positioning and corrective policy, there are few ideas as easy to get behind as equity.

It's easy to see equity in education as a matter of fairness, access, and inclusion, but that's only the case if what's being fairly accessed is a system of teaching and learning that's fluid, responsive, dynamic, neutral, alive, and able to meet the needs of an increasingly global population. For an industry struggling to get every student reading on grade level, this may be a bit too much. Equity must be judged at the individual student level rather than as a demographic. Every student experiences commonality and difference. Inherent is what's shared – that all students need knowledge and what's distinct about the individuals who make up the class.

RACISM, CLASSISM, OR JUST PLAIN IGNORANCE

We can revise and reimagine our schools, the curriculum that is incorporated, the professional pedagogy, and the technology being used. But, until it's inclusive, fair, and accessible to every student, regardless of color, social status, or academic ability, the effort continues to represent a kind of baseline for our educational goals.

10

Now What? Can We Save Our Schools?

Keith Snelson's book *Public Education Can Be Saved* calls on Americans to fix the failing public education system. Education, a key to later success, needs to be the number-one priority in this country. However, the American public education system has many systemic problems that are inhibiting children from reaching their full potential. Many of those institutional ills have been examined herein. Unfortunately, over the years the quality of public K-12 education has actually decreased. A 2007 study showed that barely one in every four high school students was ready for college level material and courses. And students of color and with limited social mobility often show a worse trend statistically. One conclusion from this data indicates that nearly 75 percent of high school students are unprepared for the demands of college course work, making them more likely to fail college courses, enter college to take remedial courses, or never enter college at all. Other studies show that only

70 percent of high school students graduate. Given the global nature of today's workplace and the level of competitiveness that exists, the conclusion is that the social and educational divide will continue to grow.

With an idea about where the educational system began, we can begin examining the problems in the system. Education was, and should be, the "great equalizer." Children should have access to good-quality education and be given the skills to have a bright future. Increasingly, we have seen this is not the case. In fact, the opposite can actually be said. Problems of "White preference" in standardized tests and the correlation between income and test scores have been examined. At-risk students and those in poverty fail at a higher rate than their more affluent peers. It is not only poor school districts that are an area of concern but also all low-income students. These children are the ones who truly need the most, but are continually the ones the system cannot reach.

To effect real change, we must accept class, race, ethnic, sexual, and emotional diversity. When asked, most Americans would agree that skin color, socioeconomic status, culture, and sexual orientation are not indicators of a person's worth. However, someone on the outside looking in might believe that America is the home of radical racism and of those who hate. It could be because of the nightly news on the television and social media sites featuring squabbling political candidates who call the country "racist, sexist, homophobic, xenophobic,

Islamophobic, perfectly willing to tear a country apart all for the sake of a political win". Millennials and Gen Zers are the generations who will provide the cure for this country's sick educational bureaucracies, which is needed to turn the system around and do right by the children that they serve.

The sad fact is that these generations are at the mercy of their own negative actions with regard to public education. Since the 1970s, public school systems have become battlegrounds for litigation and legislation, mostly designed to bring about systemic changes in guidelines for operations in a unilateral way, whether the system is needed to change or not. Parents have become far too willing to "sue" because their child was asked to conform to the rules. Instead of working to provide quality support for true academics grounded in math, science, reading, and writing, they run to the courthouse to fight against hair length and dress codes. They even fight against their child or children with regard to following rules. They litigate every aspect of the educational system.

Even with state-supported tort reform, local public school systems have spent literally billions of dollars on defending the way they operate. From claims of abuse, to bullying, to unequal access to services ... it is a never-ending process. Curiously, had these monies been spent in actually educating our children, the current downward trends being seen could possibly have been avoided.

II

It Will Take Everyone to Make Things Happen

And finally, we can no longer continue to blame the system for the failures of a few. Although it remains an essential necessity to guarantee fair and equitable access to a free and appropriate education, we have to shift our focus away from what we perceive to be *wrong* with the system and begin to accentuate what is *right* about the system. Public school systems have to address the shortage of qualified, professionally compensated educators and administrators. It *IS* a profession after all. Classroom teachers must feel supported by the system they work in. They must feel the strength of the system and never ever be left to feel alone against the forces of litigation and legislation.

Public schools must guarantee a safe place to learn and work. School safety has become a cornerstone of daily operations since the tragedy of the Columbine incident. But the school system cannot continue to be held accountable for the actions of a singular individual or a singular event. Recently, a single event of *bullying* cost a school district over $650,000 dollars! Bullying! Kids being mean to other kids! It's a natural thing, part of the very fabric developed and consistently proved through the Darwinian foundations of evolution. I do believe that school systems have a specific role in preventing as much as possible this type of behavior ... but when is the FAMILY going to begin to shoulder some of the same responsibility? Parents must be held as accountable for the systemic ills related to school safety as the school itself. Parents who are involved, engaged, and truly a willing participant in their child's education are far less likely to allow any type of negative activity from their child with respect to the school system. It's holding each other accountable – plain and simple.

We have spent decades blaming everyone and everything for the crumbling of the public education system. Since the Supreme Court handed down its landmark *Brown* case in the 1950s, where it was decided that separate BUT equal was inherently unequal, we have placed blame. We blame the failing structure of the conventional family. We blame the color of our skin. We blame our political affiliations and religious beliefs. We blame our sexual orientations and physical abilities. We blame the educators and administrators. We have learned to place blame in and on just about every aspect of society and the systemic design of the educational process. What we have NEVER done, and continue to avoid doing ... is looking introspectively! We have never, not once, blamed ourselves. We don't place blame on the breakdown of the family as an important part of the child's education. We don't accept our role in the process. Sadly, the family and the home have become almost nonexistent in the process unless litigation is involved. As parents, we have failed to accept that part of the problem lies within the structure of the home and family.

Is it a case of systemic racism? Is it classism? Do the rich kids get a better education because they are from wealthy homes? Do less affluent students receive a substandard education simply because they are poor? Research does not support that. In fact, it is clear that the educational opportunities for minorities and for those from lower socioeconomic groups are as formidable as those for all other student groups. That leaves only ignorance! As a society, we have become blatantly ignorant of the process. We have learned to blame the ills of the system on anything other than the truth. Race and ethnicity can no longer be a crutch for a child not learning. It is important to note that there is a critical need for minority teachers, teachers of color, especially male teachers of color – if for no other reason than to provide our diverse student populations with a "mirror" to who they are in the classroom. But blaming the system through the call of racism and racial disparity is tainted. And the newly designed "wokeness" of the Project 1619 curriculum is simply wrong. It is dangerous and corrupt and decidedly historically unsound. Children of color and those of diverse ethnicities must continue to receive the same opportunities for strong and relevant public education, and we must work to be inclusive and aware of these diversities. Is it racism? Is it classism? Or ... could it simply and sadly be that we are ignorant of the facts? Remember ... perception is everything!

References

Achievement Gap. (2011, August). *Education Week.* Retrieved from http://www.edweek.org/ew/issues/achievement-gap/

Bainbridge, W. L. (2002). Poverty, not race, holds back urban students. *Columbus Dispatch,* 1–5.

Balfanz, R. (2009). Can the American high school become an avenue of advancement for all? *The Future of Children,* 19(1), 17–32.

Banks, J.A. (1992). Insights on diversity: Dimensions of multicultural education. *Kappa Delta Pi,* 29(1), 12.

Banks, J.A. (1993). Multicultural education: historical development, dimensions, and practice. *Review of Research in Education,* 19, 3–49.

Banks, J.A. (1994). *An Introduction to Multicultural Education.* Boston: Allyn and Bacon.

Barton, P. (2004). Why does the gap persist? *Educational Leadership,* 62(3), 8–13.

Bell, C. (2013). Closing the achievement gap: Identifying social, societal, familial and psychological factors affecting Black students' academic performance. *The Public Purpose, (11),* 1–20.

Bethel, D. (2013). *A Comparative Perspective of Black College Males on the Achievement Gap: Implications for School Counselors.* Retrieved from http://scholarcommons.usf.edu/etd.

Boykin, A.W. (1994). *Harvesting Culture and Talent: African American Children and Educational Reform.* In R. Rossi (Ed.), *Educational Reform and At-Risk Students.* New York: Teachers College Press.

Carlson, Tucker. (2020). Fox News Channel, multiple dates, multiple shows.

Caton, M. T. (2012, August 13). Black male perspectives on their educational experiences in high school [Electronic version]. *Urban Education, 47*(6), 1055–1085. doi:10.1177/0042085912454442

Creswell, J. W. (2012). *Educational Research: Planning, Conducting, and Evaluating Quantitative and Qualitative Research* (4th ed.). New Jersey: Pearson Education.

Creswell, J. W. (2013). *Qualitative Inquiry & Research Design: Choosing Among Five Approaches* (3rd ed.). Thousand Oaks, CA: Sage, pp. 76–83.

Dallman-Jones, A. (2002). A case for separate at-risk education standards. *Journal of School Improvement, 3*(1), 34–38.

Darby, A., Mihans, R., Gonzalez, K., Lyons, M., Goldstein, J., & Anderson, K.(2007) The influence of school socioeconomic status of first-year teachers' emotions. *Research in Education, 85,* 69–78.

Davis, III, C. H. F., & Harper, S. R. (2012). They (don't) care about education: A counter narrative on Black male students' responses to inequitable schooling. *Educational Foundations,* Winter-Spring, 103–120.

Frankel, N. (1999). The importance of being earnest about standards. *The History Teacher.* 32, 401–410.

Friend, C. (2009). The influences of parental racial socialization on the academic achievement of Black children: A cultural-ecological approach. *Dissertation-University of North Carolina at Greensboro.* Retrieved from: Dissertations and Theses (Publication No. AAT 3355968).

Fryer, R.G., & Levitt, S.D. (2004). Falling behind: New evidence on the Black-White achievement gap. *Education Next,* 4(4), 1–8.

Gay, G. (2000). *Culturally Responsive Teaching: Theory, Research & Practice.* New York: Teachers College Press.

Gorski, P. (2008). The myth of the culture of poverty. *Educational Leadership,* 65(7), 32–36.

Hale, J. E. (2001). *Learning While Black: Creating Educational Excellence for African American Children.* Baltimore: The Johns Hopkins University Press.

Hardy, N. (2010). Portraits of success: Effective White female teachers of Black male middle school students. *ProQuest, LLC.,* Michigan: UMI Dissertation Publishing.

Haycock, K. (2006). No more invisible kids. *Educational Leadership,* 64(3), 38.

Hooks, B. (1992). *Talking Back: Thinking Black.* (2nd ed.). Boston: South End Press.

Hopson, L. M., & Lee, E. (2011). Mitigating the effect of family poverty on academic and behavioral outcomes: The role of school climate in middle and high school. *Children and Youth Services Review, 33,* 2221–2229.

Irizarry, J. (2009). Characteristics of the cultural deficit model. *Gale Cengage Learning: Education.com,* Retrieved from http://www.education.com

Kafele, B.K. (2009). *Motivating Black Males to Achieve in School and Life.* Virginia: ASCD.

Kunjufu, J. (2002). *Black Students. Middle Class Teachers.* Chicago: African American Images.

Kunjufu, J. (2004). *Countering the Conspiracy to Destroy Black Boys.* Chicago: African American Images.

Kunjufu, J. (2005). *Keeping Black Boys Out of Special Education.* Chicago: African American Images.

Kunjufu, J. (2011). *Understanding Black Male Learning Styles.* Chicago: African American Images.

Kunjufu, J. (2012). *There Is Nothing Wrong with Black Students.* Chicago: African American Images.

Ladson-Billings, G.J. (1994). *The Dreamkeepers: Successful Teachers of African American Students.* San Francisco: Jossey-Bass.

Ladson-Billings, G.J. (1995). Toward a theory of culturally relevant pedagogy. *American Education Research Journal, 35,* 465–491.

Lang, M. & Ford, C. A. (1992). *Strategies for Retaining Minority Students in Higher Education.* Illinois: Charles C. Thompson.

Lynch, Matthew. (2017). *18 Reasons the U.S. Educational System is Failing.*

Martin, D., & McGee, E. (2011). From the hood to being

hooded: a case study of a Black male PhD. *Journal of African American males in education, 2*(1), 46–65.

Martin, D., & McGee, E. (2011). You would not believe what I have to go through to prove my intellectual value! Stereotype management among successful Black college mathematics and engineering students. *American Educational Research Journal, 48*(6), 1347–1389.

Mazzei, L.A. (2008). Silence speaks: whiteness revealed in the absence of voice. *Teaching and Teacher Education, 25*(5), 1125–1136.

McCarthy, M. & Carter, R. (1994). *Language as Discourse: Perspectives for Language Teaching.* London: Longman Publishing.

Milner, H. R. (2007). African American males in urban schools: No excuses-teach and empower. *Theory into Practice, 46*(3), 239–246.

Milner, H. R. & Howard, T. C. (2004). Black teachers. Black students. Black communities and *Brown*: Perspectives and insights from experts. *Journal of Negro Education, 73*(3), 285–297.

National Center for Educational Information (NCEI) (2007). *Profile of Teachers in the U.S. 2007.* Washington, D.C.

National Center for Educational Statistics (2000). Retrieved from: www.nces.es.gov/nationalreportcard/states/profile/asp.

National Center for Educational Statistics. (2008). Retrieved from: www.nces.es.gov/nationalreportcard/states/profile/asp.

National Center for Educational Statistics (2013). Retrieved from: www.nces.es.gov/nationalreportcard/states/profile/asp.

Neely, A., & Wheeler, P. (2003). *Teaching African American Students: A Look at Instructional Methods and Cultural Differences.* Retrieved from College of William and Mary.

Noguera, P. A. (2003). The trouble with Black boys. The role and influence of environmental and cultural factors on the academic performance of African American males. *Urban Education, 38*(4), 431–459.

Noguera, P. A. (2014). Standing up for equity. *Instructional Leader, 27*(2), 1–2.

Oberman, I., & Symonds, K.W. (2005, January-February). What matters most in closing the gaps? *Leadership,* 8–11.

Ogbu, J. (1992). Adaption to minority status and impact on school success. *Theory into Practice, 31*(4), 287–295.

Ollernshaw, J. A., & Creswell, J.W. (2002). Narrative research: A comparison of two restoring data analysis approaches. *Qualitative Inquiry, 8,* 329–347.

Patel, K. (1994). *Multicultural Education in All-White Areas.* Aldershot: Avebury Press.

Perry, T., Steele, C., & Hilliard, A. (2003). *Young, Gifted and Black: Promoting High Achievement among African American Students.* Boston: Beacon Press.

Peters, W. (1971). *A Class Divided.* New York: Doubleday and Company.

Peters, W. (1987). *A Class Divided, Then and Now.* Connecticut: Yale University Press.

Popenoe, D. (1998). *We Are What We See: The Family Conditions for Modeling Values for Children.* Retrieved from http://www.Parenthood.library.wisc.edu/Popenoe

Schott Educational Inequity Index. (2008). *The Schott 50 State Report on Public Education and Black Males.* Retrieved from http:// www.blackboysreport.org

Schott Educational Inequity Index. (2010). *The Schott 50 State Report on Public Education and Black Males.* Retrieved from http:// www.blackboysreport.org

Schumpeter, J. (1951). *Imperialism and Social Classes: Two Essays.* Cleveland: World Publishing Company.

Silverman, M., & Studnitzer, A. (2009). The pluralistic classroom. *Teachers of Color,* 40–42. Retrieved from http://www.teachers of color.com

Spradlin, L. K. (2012). *Diversity Matters: Understanding Diversity in Schools.* (2nd ed.). California: Wadsworth/Thomson Cengage Learning.

Texas Education Agency (2011). *Accountability Manual.* Retrieved from http://ritter.tea.state.tx.us/perfreport/account/2011/manual/

Thompson, G. (2004). *Through Ebony Eyes. What Teachers Need to Know But Are Afraid to Ask about African American Students.* San Francisco: Jossey-Bass.

Thompson, G. (2007). *Up Where We Belong: Helping African American and Latino Students Rise in School and in Life.* San Francisco: Jossey-Bass.

United States Department of Education. (2012). *Black Male Teens: Moving to Success in the High School Years*. Retrieved from http://www.ed.gov/news. University of Dayton (2013).

Villegas, A.M., & Lucas, T. (2001). *Educating Culturally Responsive Teachers: A Coherent Approach*. Albany: State University of New York Press.

Villegas, A.M., & Lucas, T. (2002). Preparing culturally responsive teachers: Rethinking the curriculum. *Journal of Teacher Education*, 53(1), 20–32.

West, Cornel. (2001). *Race Matters*. New York: Vintage Books.

White, H.E. (2009). *Increasing the Achievement of African American Males*. (Report No3). Department of Research, Evaluation, and Assessment – Virginia City Beach Schools.

Wright, V. (2008). *Basic Facts about Low-Income Children*. (Report) National Center for Children in Poverty, 2009.

www.ingramcontent.com/pod-product-compliance
Lightning Source LLC
Chambersburg PA
CBHW070854220526
45466CB00005B/2001